ISBN 978-0-615-42277-0

Please forward all information/questions/requests to:
info@passtopurpose.com

Cover and layout Design:
Destiny Design & Marketing, LLC, Christie Hackley
www.iconamy.com

Readers should be aware that Internet Web sites offered as citations and/or sources for further information may have changed and/or disappeared between the time this was written and when it is read.

Keys to REBUILDING

YOUR FOUNDATION

OMARI L. PEARSON

ACKNOWLEDGEMENTS

To my wife, best friend, and advocate, I thank you for your willingness and love for me during the process. The best is yet to come! My son (and my children to come), even though you will not be able to read or understand this book for a while, I want you to know that you are my inspiration. I am writing this book so that you will have a plan of action that will take you wherever your heart desires. You have given me a greater fortitude to complete this task of leaving a legacy defined by helping others. To my grandmother, words cannot express how I love you so. I just wanted to say that I will share the goodness that you have poured into my life with the world so that others will experience the love I felt from you on a daily basis. Before anyone believed in me, you did, and for that, I am eternally grateful. Moms and Pops Sutton, you two have filled a void that I have waited nearly 25 years to receive. "All in the Family," haha! I thank you for your unconditional love and your willingness to open your hearts and pour into my life. I will always cherish every day I have had and will have with the both of you.

To my sisters - Arketa, Shavon, and Gnaun, I can not explain how honored I feel to be able to call you my sisters. Beautiful, intelligent, and loving are just a few of the words that come to mind when I try to think of a way to express how I view you. Your futures are as bright as the stars in a clear night sky. Francina - "Phat Neck," the journey has been long, but the bond has grown even stronger. Know that I love you both as an aunt and as a big sister, unconditionally. Chevelan, no mountain is too high and no valley is permanent. Always keep your head to the sky. Tamia, you have so many gifts and talents. I know that you will be a role model to many young women in the future. Commit and complete all that you touch and you will be more successful then you could ever dream. To my godparents, Dee and Janet, I thank you for removing borders by taking me across them. You will always have a special place in my heart. To my late Grandfather, I thank you. Because of you, I will always remember that you said "there is no such thing as a dumb Pearson", so apply and overcome. Dennis, I am thankful that things have come full circle in your life. You have overcome many obstacles that I will never have to face because of your strength. I love you, and I hope that we will someday have the relationship that a father and son could only dream of.

To JR, words cannot explain how proud I am of you. Stay focused! Write the vision and make it plain. Auntie "Mickey Mouse," I could not have asked for a better aunt; your love and selflessness is contagious. I will always cherish every moment I have with you. To Mama Phyllis and Dakya, I thank you for your unconditional love and support. To Billy, Lewis, Mark, Lornzo, Anthony, and Kevin time has turned friendship into brotherhood, and for that I am grateful. To Pastor Joel, I thank you for your daily encouragement and prayers, you truly have been a blessing in my life. To John Bryant, your life has been a daily reminder that life is so much bigger then "I." To Isiah, thank you for your wisdom and support in seasons where I needed it most. To every person from Uncles to Aunts, to my brothers-sisters, to my cousins: I want you to know that I love you all. For anyone I left out, please blame it on my head and not my heart.

To all my mentors, friends, and family I thank you for helping me discover my purpose.

TABLE OF CONTENTS

FOREWORD

In 1986, I lost the most important figure in my life: my mother. However, because of her death, my life would change in ways I never would have imagined. I would learn very quickly that every negative situation potentially positions you for a future blessing, if you allow it to occur. Whether through the birth of a child, or sudden success, the sun always seems to follow the darkest nights. For me, my sunrise came in the form of a medical malpractice lawsuit that would position me to inherit money at the age of 13, and my life would go from that of a city kid to that of a trust fund heir. There was only one problem: I was not prepared for this new life. Because of this lack of preparation, I would learn some really hard lessons about money, friends, family, and life.

The wealth that came as a result of losing my mother caused me to create a life based upon fear that to this day I fight daily. Poverty mindsets come in many different forms, and for me it would take the form of financial ignorance combined with a fear of losing people, topped off with a desire to help others; it is a dangerous combination for anyone to mix, let alone a 13-year old. It is for that very reason I write this book, so that those who find themselves in a completely different position as a result of death, graduation, wealth, athletic success, or any other form of instant manifestation can stand tall without being limited by their own lack of knowledge. Let this book serve as a foundational blueprint for you; make sure that whatever blessing comes your way does not just brighten your life, but the life of those around you.

In life, we practice sports, we study for exams, we train physically, and we study to show ourselves continued improvement. However, for some reason, we overlook the importance of learning how to find purpose in everything we have, whether that is wealth, education, our own obstacles, etc.

The areas I felt a deep need to include in this first book are: Accountability, Vision, Purpose, Dreams, Your Team, Your Surroundings, and Your Foundation. These are just a few of the areas that I now know the importance of after experiencing many difficult life lessons. I will include some of those lessons in this book, not to tell you all of my business, but rather so that you hopefully can learn from my mistakes and choose to apply wisdom to the knowledge I hope you gain from this book.

My goal with this book is to give you a clear blueprint for how to establish your goals and solidify your foundation, while bringing together a team that will help you form a plan to overcome any obstacles standing in the way of letting you live out your purpose.

I know this book will show you how to establish a team to help you eliminate your weaknesses by allowing their strengths to become yours. This is what author Napoleon Hill called the "Master Mind Theory." It allows your dreams to become a healthy functioning vision that has all the necessary parts to bring both your dreams and goals to manifestation.

I dedicate this book to those persons that statistics say are not supposed to be able to overcome the world's obstacles and life's inevitable circumstances. With a clear plan and a 100% effort, all things are possible to the person who believes. No matter how cliché it may sound, "If you can believe, you can achieve." My goal is to give you a few tools that can help you better position yourself toward the path of success and dream fulfillment.

For everyone who has ever shaped my life, I thank you,

because without you, my dreams would never have had the fire to burn to completion. Every person who comes into your life either shapes you positively or motivates you to dig deeply to find the strength to overcome their negative limitations that try to influence you.

CHAPTER ONE
ACCOUNTABILITY

Accountability (n): the state of being account-able, liable, or answerable [1]

From the time you are born till the time you die, you will be accountable to someone; whether it is your parents, boss, mortgage holder, car note lender, your family, or even yourself, you will be accountable!

Many young adults have a lack of understanding as to why parents (guardians) are important to their future success. One of the many jobs a parent has is to hold his children accountable for their actions. This is why it is important that children listen and respect their parents, even when they disagree with what their parents are saying. Lack of accountability is like having a beautiful house with all the beautiful trimmings, only to find out after living in it for a while that the foundation is unstable.

Accountability is the foundation for the fulfillment of your dreams. As young adults mature and begin to enter into a more independent lifestyle, they are also entering into greater levels of self-accountability. That is why parents often say, "Do not rush your life, enjoy it, because soon enough you will have a chance to make your own decisions."

Every man and woman on this Earth has responsibilities, but for some reason, as you become an adult, those responsibilities become more glaring and more mandatory then they were as an adolescent. The more people, family, employees, etc. that you have depending on you, the greater the stress can be.

Many kids dream of having the big house, the exotic car, and the ability to travel and go when they want and where they want. Most never take into account that many who reach that level of wealth often times have very little time to be involved in leisure activities. Most of their time is spent with things that either move their estate/wealth forward, or attempting to prevent it from going backwards.

The more money one has often leads to a greater level of accountability.

The phrase "more money, more problems" is a true statement. When money comes in, you'd better have an inner circle of people who will hold you accountable. Why? Statistics show that seventy percent of all people who receive wealth fast, whether inherited or received suddenly, lose their money.

Athletes, chief executive officers (CEOs), actors, and many others have seen how a lack of accountability can affect a person's finances negatively. You have to learn and understand that every situation you go through gives you a chance to gain a deeper understanding, knowledge, and experience. Before you begin to see the reward for your commitment, you need to make sure that you are prepared. How you apply your understanding will either be a positive or negative decision

The more money, the more responsibilities you have.

I remember that when I inherited my mother's estate, I had not been trained, nor was I prepared to receive it; therefore, when the time came, I was overwhelmed. As a result, I had to rely on lawyers, bankers, and family members to make the best choices for me. How was I to know if they had my best interests at heart, or if they were simply recommending things because of the fees they could charge? I had to trust them. "For that reason, I strongly believe that banks should develop stronger financial education programs for the trust-fund beneficiaries for whom they provide services."

Looking back, there are a lot of things I would do differently, none of which could be blamed solely on the bank. If I had spent as much time reading books on finance as I did playing video games, I would have been more educated and able to speak with a higher level of authority and understanding. If I did not want to take the time to read, I could have bought audio books. You see, if there is a will, there is a way. I just did not take the time to find out or to look for it. Our society loves to blame everyone except the one who has the ultimate power, "YOU!"

When you read a book, you may not agree or understand all the author's opinions, but by reading their opinions (writing), you will begin to build your IQ based on your needs and their recommendations. The knowledge you lean from reading will hold you accountable by removing the excuse not ever being informed.

The lack of accountability ultimately pushed me into a position that I wish I never would have had to endure. However, because of it, I now have a company that focuses on helping people have a greater level of accountability not only with their dreams, but also with their finances. It is often said that you find out who you are when you reach rock bottom. It is my hope that this book will be able to help others before their negative financial and/or life decisions place them in the abyss. I have always been a helper and one to share any information I received. Therefore, with "Passion To Purpose, LLC," I hope to help people through books, simulations, and mentoring.

Wisdom (is) the quality or state of being wise;

knowledge of what is true or right coupled with
just judgment as to action; sagacity, discernment,
or insight$_2$

Knowledge (is) the body of truths or facts accu-
mulated in the course of time$_3$

Wisdom gives you the ability to take knowledge and make a good decision. As you grow, you must surround yourself with people who have no hidden agendas, but who will help and direct you so that you can prosper in all that you do.

OUR HURTS

It is funny how life shapes our judgments and decisions. Every time we share ourselves with someone who hurts us, a wall is formed that tries to block the next person who wants to help us reach our dreams. When someone close to you hurts you, a wall is built, but for this reason, you have to educate yourself and understand the source from which the disappointment came. Was it done to hurt you, or was it simply a mistake? Was he or she trying to help? Why should you forgive that person and move on? These questions are very important, and they will allow you the freedom to choose to forgive someone whom you may not have ever wanted to forgive, so that you can focus your energy on reaching your dreams and goals. Remember, you only have so much energy to use everyday; for that reason alone, forgiveness is very important, so you can focus your energy on things to come instead of the past pulling you backwards.

POWER OF MONEY

Money carries with it an emotional value. It is neither good nor bad; it only takes on the shape of its owner. Therefore, when people with money are nice, it is because their inner core of who they are is that of a nice person. The opposite holds true if someone is not nice. The same could be said if you encounter someone who uses his money to try to control you or other people you may know.

Money is a neutral tool that simply takes on the identity you give it. How you decide to spend it, save it, or share it is determined solely by you, not by the money.

Money is a major reason you should have a team around you that holds you accountable, to prevent your issues from becoming liabilities in your long-term life/financial goals.

You must make sure your team holds you accountable at all times.

For every decision I make, I know that the team of people I have surrounding me will hold me accountable. In addition, my inner circle is highly competent in their understanding of financial matters. I have successful business owners, accountants, lawyers, entertainers, visionaries, and others whose opinions I can use when I have a decision to make.

MILITARY

The military is one of the most widely held accountable organizations in the world. From newly-enlisted solders to generals, the chain of command is in place so that every decision is made and executed in one heartbeat. Its amazing to me that while the military is a volunteer organization, each member still must be accounted for. If not, that soldier is considered absent without leave.

Now, if an organization that holds the majority of its members, who volunteered their services, to that level of accountability, why then would a child who lives in a house, in which he/she pays for nothing, not understand that it is his/her duty to report to and do whatever his/her parents ask of him/her (within the bounds of reason)? It is the easiest task that child will ever have. Yet, every day

These are the questions you should be asking yourself long before you ever graduate from college.

children and youth complain or rebel against these minor levels of accountability, which only serve to prepare them for their future self-accountability.

Accountability is what keeps things in proper order. It is what will help you eliminate any decision that could lead you off course from accomplishing your dreams. Accountability is the glue that keeps your dream together.

DIFFERENT LEVELS OF ACCOUNTABILITY

When your plumbing is not working correctly, you do not call the cable company. Why? The answer is simple: The cable company cannot help. Therefore, why do we rely on people who have never gone where we are trying to go to plan our route? They can help you research, but that is all they can do, because they are just as new to what you are trying to accomplish as you are.

If you are going to be the first in your family to graduate college and you are looking for advice, who should you ask?

The bigger the decision, the more I research.

If you ask yourself the questions listed above, it will help you begin to assemble a team of people who are qualified to help you answer questions that only someone with experience can provide. Remember, you do not call the cable guy when your plumbing is not working correctly.

When someone gives you advice, you should listen, even if it sounds crazy to you. Afterwards, research and check to see if it is valid. If it is not, throw it away and move on. Everyone may not have all the answers, but one word could be the missing piece to the puzzle you are trying to solve.

When you are being advised and guided, you must have a standard to make sure you know that the advice you are receiving is good. For that reason alone, I read books, watch shows, and even still to this day have to refer to others for advice.

I have learned that accountability, although annoying at times, is one of the biggest keys to being successful. I try to keep people around me who are able to keep me on task and who will make sure I am not wasting time.

TIME

Time is the reason why accountability is so important. Each one of us has two events that are guaranteed in our lifetimes: We will be born, and we will die. However, it is what we do in between those events that will determine how we will be remembered. Accountability makes sure that you leave a positive footprint on your journey through life.

If someone is holding you accountable, keep them close. They are rarer and more valuable then any diamond, because they are willing to tell you the truth no matter whether you want to hear it or not.

*Truth (is) conformity with fact or reality; verity*₄

In most successful organizations, there is a clear and present chain of accountability that allows the organization to be successful. Your life is no different. If you are a teenager, you are the president of your life, but your parents are the CEOs; therefore, you have to maintain effective communication so that your boss is able to help steer you when needed.

EXAMPLE:

Athletic Accountability Chain of Command:
- Owners hold general managers accountable
- General Managers hold coaches accountable
- Coaches hold players accountable
- Players hold each other accountable

Business Accountability Chain of Command:
- CEOs hold presidents accountable
- Presidents hold vice-presidents accountable
- Vice-Presidents hold managers accountable
- Managers hold workers accountable

ACCOUNTABILITY CHANGES OVER TIME

In the beginning, your responsibilities are greater, but as you move closer to your dream, you will begin to have different people who fill certain roles and who will make you more productive.

They say that the more things change, the more they stay the same. The same is true when you enter the workforce. Instead of your parents as your CEOs, now your boss or supervisor takes that position. If you have your own business, you are accountable to your customers. Anyone who is successful is accountable. There is no way around it.

This is why the United States of America does not just have one branch of government. It is why Great Britain has parliament. Accountability is a piece in the puzzle that will allow you to maximize your time so that you reach your dreams and goals – balance.

"Accountability breeds response-ability"
—Stephen R. Covey[5]

So when doubt, fear, and disbelief try to rise within you, you need people in your circle who will tell you to stop being a victim and take authority of your life. We all need that from time to time.

PERSONAL NOTES CHAPTER ONE

_____

_____

_____

_____

_____

_____

_____

_____

_____

_____

_____

_____

_____

_____

_____

_____

_____

_____

_____

_____

_____

CHAPTER TWO
VISION

Vision (n): the act or power of anticipating that which will or may come to be[6]

Often times, we find ourselves looking back on how time has gone by, wishing we could either undo or relive those moments again. In those moments, we realize how precious and special our time here on Earth is. For as long as I can remember, I have always been a dreamer, often to where I could foresee and believe things that very few people around me could. It was not until recently that I realized that my dreams were nothing more than tools to propel me to action; however, I had to be careful not to allow my dreams to become fantasies. Many dreamers miss their opportunity to move their dreams into reality because they never develop a plan of action. If you can see it, you can believe it. Then it is easier to achieve it. Notice the word "easier," not "easy."

THE BEGINNING

I have had the pleasure of traveling to Europe, Africa, and South America, but before any of that, I traveled in my bedroom as a child. My room was no bigger then 8x10. I had enough room to fit a full-size bed and a dresser, but to me, it was all the space I needed to travel and dream about things that I had seen on television or overheard others talking about. It was there that I began to dream.

Many people often wish they had more siblings. Some wish they had a brother, others a sister. I do not know how that would have affected my dreams, but one thing I know for certain is that I never wanted others to interfere with my dreaming process. Many dreamers today allow others to interfere with their dreams by voicing opinions that contradict their dreams. If I had more siblings living with me as a child, I may not have dreamt as much. Like many children, I dreamt about having brothers and sisters. I dreamt about living in a better neighborhood. By dreaming, I learned how to make the most of situations. This is an important quality for all dreamers, because not all dreams will come to reality, but you must learn and move forward until you reach your goal.

Dreamers never stop dreaming until all their dreams either come to pass or pass them by.

I often dreamt about so many different things, that when opportunities arose, I was ready to make a decision. Your vision must be able to always see the glass as an opportunity for something to drink, whether it is half-full or almost empty. Every dream must be nurtured to realty. I would think about dreams for days, months, and even years.

Always value whatever you have and just because you can dream it, does not mean you have to buy it.

Therefore, when the time came to shift into the manifestation of my dreams, all I had to do was review my plan of action. Sadly enough for me, many times I never wrote my plan of action, and when the doors opened to allow my dreams to become realty, I lost focus. Your vision has to be 20/20 before your dreams come to pass. If not, you will inevitably position yourself to make ill-advised decisions that could have been prevented.

I did not understand that even with a clear plan of action, I could never satisfy all my dreams. Some dreams are to be passed on to the next generation to carryout. If not, life would be an endless journey, and there is not enough money or time in the world to satisfy that kind of quest.

When your vision is out of sorts, you lose perspective and immediately you begin to see things out of context. Without goals, you lose the ability to reflect and focus on the big picture. Someone once told me that it is easy to tell a person's goals by simply looking at where and how they spend their money.

Money represents your time. For example, if you were to inherit money as opposed to working for it, the money would have a different value for you as opposed to if you had earned it. I often talk with youth and I ask them to give me an example of a typical week's spending. They look at me and wonder why am I asking such an odd question, but yet, they still share their spending habits with me. I listen eagerly, but more often then not, they never mention anything of value.

Value - relative worth, merit, or importance[7]

VISION OF BILLIONAIRES:

What do Bill Gates and Oprah Winfrey have in common? Wealth! Not only do they have more than enough, but they were willing to sacrifice and correct their visions to allow their companys to grow into industry leaders.

Do what you have to do, so you can do what you want to do.

Bill Gates withdrew from Harvard, one of the most prestigious universities in the world, to focus on his dream. Oprah had to overcome many obstacles to become one of the most recognizable names in the world. Both Bill Gates and Oprah Winfrey had to focus their energy while sacrificing much to position their companies to become industry leaders.

I strongly believe that whatever you spend most of your time doing brings either a successful result or a negative reward. It is up to you; not your mother, father, mentor, or friends, it is up to you.

> *Success (is) the favorable or prosperous termination of attempts or endeavors[8]*

> *A reward is something given or received in return or recompense for service, merit, hardship, etc.[9]*

When your vision is focused, you are like a horse with blinders on, never looking to the left or the right, but only connecting with those things that allow you to move closer to the goal line of your dreams.

When questions arise such as, "Why should I stay in school?" the answer should be simple: "My goals require me to educate myself." "Why should I not be involved in gangs?" Easy, "It's counterproductive to me reaching my dreams." When you attach something tangible to your dreams, you give them more value.

Despite having a plan of action, you must always be prepared for the unexpected.

Many successful people were motivated by how hard their parents had to work to provide the basic necessities of life. They decided that they would not live the lives their parents had to endure. Their parents work, or lack of, was the tangible asset that kept them focused when their failures and obstacles arose. No matter what your situation may be, you have to find something to dangle in front of you that will keep you accountable and motivated.

VIEWPOINT

Whenever you look at anything, always look at it from several angles: front, back, side, bottom, and inside. By doing that, you will be able to recognize the value of what you are analyzing has in respect to your dreams. Never just accept something without viewing all the angles. A man once said to me: **"You can never live on another man's understanding. You must be willing to find out for yourself."**

Understanding your situation not only allows you to appreciate it, but it also gives you added motivation for those times when you would rather not be working towards your dream. Always challenge yourself. Challenging yourself will be one of the most important keys to unlocking your dreams.

Education has a major role and purpose, but without proper planning, it leaves you with an empty feeling. Thousands of college students graduate from college without knowing what their next move will be. Why? They had goals without a plan, or maybe they just were never informed that you must always have a plan of action.

Words without proof are worthless, but words with action (proof) are priceless.

A plan of action takes you from the status of an average person with a dream, to a person with a goal/plan, passion, and a road map on how to get there. Passion and direction are a dangerous combination with which to be armed.

Have you ever tried to tell a friend something that he did not believe? How successful were you, once he made up his mind? Why? When someone makes up their mind, it is a lot harder to sway them into believing you. You must educate yourself on your goals the same way you study for a test. The only difference is that this test carries a long-term grade. Then, when people voice their opinions, you will not be as easily swayed toward changing your dreams, because you did your homework and have the knowledge of what it will take to bring your dream to pass.

BEING PREPARED

You cannot afford to not know whether you need a certain grade point average, or if you need three years of experience upon graduating from school to enter the career field of your dreams. You must already know. Why? Because time is the most valuable commodity you have, and any minute spent not living your dream is a minute you will never have an opportunity to relive.

You must research so that you can have an understanding of what it takes to reach your dreams. That way, when opportunities present themselves, you are in a position to take advantage of them. When I was in college and playing basketball, I prided myself on knowing all the positions and responsibilities for each play. Why, you may ask? Because I wanted to play! Therefore, I figured that if I understood all the positions' responsibilities, I would have a higher chance at playing time. When you want something to come about, you must position yourself appropriately. Never focus on only one angle, because you may miss an opportunity that could have moved you closer to another dream. Did knowing all the positions help? Not at that time, but it does now, without question! You never know when the skills you are acquiring now will be needed later in life.

Prepare not only for today but weigh it for tomorrow.

Do not be the one who misses the forest because of the trees. Be the eagle that sees everything: the forest, the mountains, and the river. Prepare!

Be careful not to surround yourself with dream thieves.

> *Thief (is) a person who steals, esp. secretly or*
> *without open force; one guilty of theft or lar-*
> *ceny*[10]

You know the thieves of which I speak: those people who have no vision, nor do they have a plan. They simply live for the moment, missing opportunities that could change their lives forever. They only see the trees, missing the beautiful mountains behind them.

Henry Ford was the founder of the Ford Motor Company, and is considered the father of the assembly line. As the owner of Ford Motor Company, he became one of the richest and best-known people in the world (Wikipedia.com). His definition of obstacles: **"Those frightful things you see when you take your eyes off your goals."**[11]

Are you disciplined enough to stay focused? Are you confident enough that when the winds blow, your house will stand? Make sure that you are! Your dreams depend on it.

PERSONAL NOTES CHAPTER TWO

_____

_____

_____

_____

_____

_____

_____

_____

_____

_____

_____

_____

_____

_____

_____

_____

_____

_____

_____

_____

CHAPTER THREE
PURPOSE

Purpose (n): the reason for which something exists or is done, made, or used[12]

Every day, thousands of children are born, each one with a gift and purpose that will make the world a better place. There's only one problem: life. It has a way of intervening and taking people off track, causing us to settle for whatever comes our way instead of living "A Purpose Driven Life," as Pastor Rick Warren's aptly titled book calls it.

Life has a way of causing people to give up on their dreams because of unexpected responsibilities that are the result of our choices. Having a child can be one of the biggest and best events to ever happen in your life. However, in the same light, having a child prematurely could change a dreamer's life forever. That is why adults tell youth to remain abstinent; not to remove pleasure, but to ensure that they will have an opportunity to enjoy life

You can not have passion without purpose being either there or at the door waiting to enter.

without the restrictions that sex can bring if entered into prematurely. Whenever a child is born, each parent's life is changed forever. Most would agree that one of the jobs a parent has is to promote and help his children reach their purpose.

When we are born, there is something in us that searches for answers. Watch babies; they are constantly searching, through a process of elimination and exploration, to find out how their bodies and their new environment work. As long as we live, that search will never end.

Some people try to fill the curiosity of life with sports, work, education, family, and many other things that can not completely satisfy one's self in the same way that discovering their purpose can. People have gone lifetimes without ever discovering why they are here on Earth, feeling as if they were missing something. Life without purpose is like a dog chasing its tail, constantly running, but never going anywhere.

For this reason, I think families should come together as often as possible to do personal and family evaluations. It would allow them to hold each other accountable, and allow them to evaluate and see the changes that each member has undergone since the previous meeting. Your home should be a place where things can be dealt with and fixed without the public or peers ever knowing. The home should be sacred ground. It should be a place where dreams and plans are built and solidified.

It bewilders me to see how family issues have become something that we share with the public. Truth be told, every household has issues that needs to be addressed. Our culture has begun to focus on other peoples' issues while forgetting or simply overlooking their own. For this very reason, families must begin to have a greater level of transparency among one another. Communication allows purpose to be identified by all; and, if the lines of communication are open, you will have a higher chance of reaching your goals, whether through counsel or financing.

FAMILY

In six years of marriage, I have found out things about myself in ways that I thought I had already understood. I had to be honest with myself. Therefore, the Cosby Show fantasy was quickly removed, and I found that just like anything else that had purpose, it would take work, time, and patience. I had to reflect on issues that I had put on the back burner. When you live with someone daily, all of your hidden hurts and pains eventually come to the surface. I had and still have a lot of issues that easily could have prevented me and my wife from completing our purpose together. Anger, pride, lying, lust, family, money and many other things tried to derail me from my purpose, both personally and within my marriage.

Whether it is your wife, friends, or family members, it is important that you have someone who will be honest and real with you, no matter how you feel or how you receive what he/she has to say. You should always have a team of people who will give you an honest evaluation of how you are moving towards or away from your purpose. This is why your purpose is so important, because it brings a clear understanding when it is accompanied by a solid team and foundation. Without a purpose, you have nothing to measure against in regards to what is on task or is not on task. You have to ask yourself, does this line up with my plan or not? Just because it appears to be successful does not mean it is your purpose. You have to be careful that you do not become sidetracked by things that ultimately will not lead to the fulfillment of your purpose.

I thought basketball was my purpose, so after having success and reaching all but one of my goals in having an NBA playing career, I felt as if I was completely empty. Why? Because I thought I was already operating in my purpose. Wow! What a shocker! It is like someone working 20 years at a job, only to be fired. You give your blood, sweat, and tears to a company, only to have it blow up in your face. I endured injuries, grueling hours in the gym, and multiple hours on the track, but I still had not reached what I thought was my life's purpose. Basketball was just a key that would equip me with the necessary tools to fulfill my true purpose in life. I was on a road heading towards my purpose, acting as if I had already reached my destination. Basketball was just preparation. When you are on the way to your purpose, it is like being on a journey in which every road presents a lesson that can either push you forward or hold you back. It is all in how you view the situation that will determine your end results.

HOW TO FIND YOUR PURPOSE

Ask yourself: "What would I do for free?" Is it helping people, making people laugh, teaching people, or sharing what you know? All those qualities are possible indicators that can lead to the discovery of your ultimate purpose.

When you commit to your dreams, there is nothing else.

For as long as I can remember, I dreamt about playing for the Chicago Bulls, hearing the announcer say my name and city in the starting lineup. It is what motivated me to go to the gym at 5:45 a.m. It is what sent me to North Bridgeton, Maine, and then on to York, Pennsylvania. Why? I was in search of my purpose through my dream. Many people thought I was crazy to do all the things I did, but I believed that it was a part of a bigger plan to help me reach my goal. I knew that I wanted to be a professional basketball player. However, I must admit that there were times when I thought that maybe what I was doing was crazy, but no matter, I had come too far to give up.

Oftentimes we think that our dreams are our purpose, and oftentimes they are not.

HOW TO FIND YOUR PURPOSE

In college, being "all in" meant I had to give up my summers to work on my skills. Being "all in" is what led me to transfer my senior year. Ultimately, it allowed me to play in an NBA summer league as a starter. It is also what sent me to Argentina, which is one of the most beautiful countries in the world. Finally, it took me to my last stop on the basketball train - San Antonio Texas, to work out with the San Antonio Spurs.

Always enjoy your success, because in life everything has a beginning and an end.

After all that, I felt just as empty as if I had not been able to reach any of those milestones. Why? I thought I had reached my purpose and fulfilled it. I thought about what was going to be next. If that was my purpose, there was nothing left to accomplish. I did not understand that basketball was only the key that started the vehicle; I still had to drive to the destination.

When I look at successful people, I see talent, work ethic, positioning, gifts, and many other attributes that have allowed them to be successful. However, despite all those different attributes and their successes, those people can still feel as empty as if they were not having any success at all. Why? Because, success does not mean you are operating in your purpose. Purpose is what completes you. It brings a joy that money could never buy.

FIND YOUR FIRST LOVE

As long as I can remember I have loved helping others through whatever knowledge I had acquired, no matter how big or small. As a child, one of my goals was to blaze a trail so that people could walk on my shoulders as they were starting their journeys towards their goals. Once basketball was removed, I had to find my first love. What was your first love? Some of you reading this book will

No matter how bleak a situation, there is always light if you look hard enough.

have to search harder then others, but when you find your first love, you will begin to rediscover your passions, which will help lead to your purpose.

ROCK BOTTOM

It is said that at your lowest moment, you will find out who you really are. I would also like to add to that statement, and say that in those moments, its when your purpose will begin to become so clear that you will have no questions as to whether it is your purpose or not. It is in that place that your dreams will begin to align with your purpose, and you will not allow anything else to interfere. No statements, all you will accept is genuine hard evidence of a success that only your purpose could bring.

Successful people understand how to create patterns of success.

When farmers plant apples, they do not expect oranges. Likewise, you should not accept anything less than the fulfillment of your purpose in whatever task you are involved. If you are operating in your purpose, you will have a peace and joy that will not be able to be explained in words. It will surpass all natural understanding.

Ask yourself these questions:

* What am I doing today that will shape the world around me tomorrow?

* Am I enjoying today's purpose while I prepare for tomorrow?

CONTRACTS

In a court of law, a contract is a legal binding agreement, which if established correctly under the law of that state, holds all parties accountable. Below I have a contract, and if you are serious about reaching your goals, I would like you to sign and read daily. You must have someone (e.g., an adult) to witness your signature and sign it with you, who will hold you accountable to the contract that you are signing today.

CONTRACT:

I, _____, do hereby agree that I will only attach and allow those things that are attached to my purpose to be a part of my day-to-day activities. If anyone is not helping me to move forward, I will wish them the best, but I will ask that they either change their stance or remove themselves altogether. I will attach myself to people who are purpose-motivated so that we can move forward as a team in order to complete the task of making the world a better place than it was before I was born.

Signed on this ____day of ____in the year of ____.

Signed by: _____

Witnessed by: _____

PERSONAL NOTES CHAPTER THREE

_____

_____

_____

_____

_____

_____

_____

_____

_____

_____

_____

_____

_____

_____

_____

_____

_____

_____

_____

_____

CHAPTER FOUR
DREAMS

Dream (n): is a wild fancy hope$_{13}$

W hen people hear the word "dream," many ideas enter their minds. To me, no idea is greater than the dream that millions of immigrants and slaves alike shared upon arriving on the shores of the United States of America. Many of those who arrived on these shores never had a chance to see their dreams come true; however, their sacrifices provided for the generations that followed.

On the 28th of August in 1963, Martin Luther King, Jr. gave a speech that spoke to the dreams of those who had come before him and would live after his death. His speech expressed the purpose of everything he had endured up to that point.

Dreams shift mindsets, and mindsets control environments. So, if you can shift minds, you can ultimately shift environments.

To not dream is to rob future generations of the opportunity to decide whether they want to reap from the harvest of their forefathers' sweat, blood, and tears. That is why you set your goals high, so that even if you fall short, the next generation that follows you will be in a better position than you were when you started your journey. Your dreams become the road that the next generation has to follow if the plan is clear.

PROTECT YOUR DREAMS

Your dreams are sacred. You have to guard and protect your dreams to the best of your ability. You cannot share your dreams with just anyone. First, many will not be able to understand your dreams, and second, many will try to discourage and add doubt to your thoughts.

Doubt, fear, and disbelief are three of the many toxins that can hamper your dreams from coming to fruition. You have to know that your dreams are yours, and no one will ever believe in your dreams like you. It feels very good to have people support your dreams, but more often than not, you will have to be your own biggest supporter.

There are no shortcuts to reaching any dream worth fulfilling.

That is why your dreams need to be deeply planted inside you so that no one can come and cast doubt or fear on to them. That goes for family, friends, and mentors. You have to settle it in your mind that you will become victorious, no matter the cost or effort needed. How? Working hard, favor, and strategic alignments will be your keys to reaching what many will see as impossible. There should not be anything to distract you from your dreams; it's simply all or nothing.

Are you "all in?"

A TWISTED PERSPECTIVE

Before basketball was ever a goal for me, I wanted to help others become successful. I was the kid that was excited to babysit, carry the groceries, or offer my opinion on all manners of things. I loved the feeling that I had when I was able to help someone reach or complete a task. Somehow, when I became involved in basketball, I lost focus on that pleasure I once had. I forgot about my original dream. It was not until four years after I finished playing sports that I began to remember that passion I once possessed.

There was only one problem with my gift: I only had joy if others found joy in me helping them. Many people have gifts and talents that are abused for that very reason. Instead of simply enjoying the fact of moving within their gifts or talents, they allow others to dictate whether they can enjoy them or not. When you realize that your gifts can give you pleasure, whether people like it or not, this is when you will begin to experience the joy that few people have ever been able to experience.

Drug addicts cannot counsel other drug addicts to quit drugs if they are still using. The same philosophy applied to me, in that I could not try to help others if I was not first happy with myself. Now, when I speak, I do it from the heart and tell the truth, whether people want to hear it or not.

I could not counsel others to make myself feel good. I had to first feel good regardless, because at the end of the day, not one person should ever have the power to control your joy. Nor should you allow people or money to influence your joy. Your dreams and passions should be your motivation, regardless of your paycheck. Your dreams should be able to bring about an excitement in your inner being for what the day may hold.

When you are giving back, always check your motives, because if they are not pure, it will prevent you from being productive in mentoring good leaders.

Whenever you dream, make sure your dream is not determined by a hole that you have in yourself. There is nothing wrong with wanting to help others, but make sure that you deal with any personal issues you may have before you start giving advice from your empty place. There is nothing wrong with helping others while you are healing, but you must make sure you are strong enough to give help before you start speaking.

If you are mentoring anyone, understand that talk is cheap. You must live a life that reflects your words. You never want to be accused of being a hypocrite. You never want your integrity to be questioned by those you are trying to help, because a character flaw can be a major hindrance in helping others.

I am not writing this book off of another man's knowledge or research alone. I have lived this. I have made good and bad choices. The only difference is that I have had an opportunity to correct mine. You may or may not be as lucky, so make the most of your choices now.

PERSONAL NOTES CHAPTER FOUR

_____

_____

_____

_____

_____

_____

_____

_____

_____

_____

_____

_____

_____

_____

_____

_____

_____

_____

_____

_____

_____

_____

CHAPTER FIVE
TEAM

*Team (n) a number of persons associated in
some joint action[14]*

As a former athlete and currently a businessman, to me, the word "team" carries a number of different meanings. Some were positive and some were negative, depending on the level of success we had as a team, and how I was able to partner with my teammates during the process. Any team worth its salt is bonded together through situations that bring them together to resolve a task and/or overcome a situation.

Whether you look at successful teams or companies, you will see that they all share one common characteristic: unity.

My definition of team: many different personalities and skills, coming together to form one seamless unit to accomplish one single task.

*Unity - an undivided or unbroken completeness
or totality with nothing wanting[15]*

As you begin the journey to fulfilling your dreams and goals, you will quickly see that you will need others. This is not a mystery, but it is more of an inevitable outcome to the process that we all have to undertake in our journeys to fulfilling our dreams. Somewhere between the start and finish, there will be an obstacle that you cannot tackle on your own. You will need help from others.

"I" is only one letter, yet "team" is made up of four.
Whether it is advice, direction, or maybe even a key connection, you will need someone. "I" is never a powerful as "team."

What you do from the beginning to the completion of your journey of fulfilling your dream has to be strategic, honest, and done with a clear and present purpose.

CONNECTIONS

Imagine what an endorsement from Oprah Winfrey, Michael Jordan, or Bill Gates could do to help you in your journey of reaching your dreams. Even though you may not have a direct connection to any of the names listed above, you may have access to others, whom if you were to ask, would be excited about the opportunity to assist you.

OPRAH WINFREY

If your dream is to be involved in entertainment media, who could be a better advocate for you than Oprah Winfrey? She could direct you to the college majors necessary to be successful. She could connect you with companies that would allow you to gain the necessary experience to accelerate your learning curve. In your city, there are thousands of Oprahs. Of course, they may not have the same level of influence, but they have an understanding and some relationships that could open similar doors, just as if she were to do it herself. You have to seek those people out in your city and ask them to mentor, direct, and guide you. I promise you that if you have good mentors, it will be so much easier to attain your dreams.

Your team should be well-seasoned in the field that you are trying to enter/reach. Act as though you are bringing together a team to win a game. You do not want people who cannot help you win. The same rule applies in building a successful team of people around you. Research and make sure every member can bring something valuable to your dream team.

Never burn bridges or towns, because on the way home you will probably have to put out the fire.

Please do not mistake what I am saying to be a microwave process. Not at all! All things have a process, but you can eliminate unnecessary detours on your journey by surrounding yourself with people who have already accomplished what you are trying to reach.

When you awaken every morning, there is a process for you to complete before you leave the house. You have to begin to surround yourself with process fillers, which are people who have already been through the same or a similar process to the one you are going through now. If you can form something like a Henry Ford assembly line team of individuals who all have an understanding or knowledge about what you are trying to accomplish, you can position yourself to become better prepared and ready to move forward. The United States of America was built upon this simple philosophy. The different government branches come together to make better decisions, because they know that one organization or leader could never know as much as several groups.

BILL GATES

Microsoft is one of the most well-known and respected companies in the world today. How did Bill Gates arrive at where he is today? Now, I ask you to please understand the question I just proposed. I am not referring to his net worth, which most people would agree is unbelievable. That is just the reward for assembling a team that bought into his vision, and financial reward followed as a result. People who only rely on their ideas and goals limit themselves to only one strategy, one thought, and one outcome. Teams have several strategies and several thoughts, thereby giving them a better chance of making quality decisions.

MICHAEL JORDAN

When you give up yourself for the benefit of the team, the team usually prospers more than if you had not given up anything at all.

Michael Jordan is easily one of the most well-known names and faces around the world. However, even as talented as he was, his success did not peak until he had the right pieces around him to eliminate his opponent's ability to focus in on just him. When he averaged over 35 points a game, he had all the individual awards, but it was not until he had a team of people around him that he became known as the greatest basketball player ever.

Great leaders relinquish their individual power, control, and glory so that the team may be able to shine. How would the world view Michael Jordan if he never won a championship? That is a question that he will never have to answer, because he had a team around him, and championships ensued. You do not have to be a rocket scientist to know that by giving up some of his individual glory, he still received more individual glory. Now that is a principle!

If you never give up anything, how will you ever have room for more?

Harpo Studios, Microsoft, and the Jordan brand all share similar key qualities that brought them success. All of them show that individual skills are needed, but that when you apply your individual skills with a team of great minds, success follows. Teamwork equals success! If you can assemble a team that buys into your vision, you will have a chance to be a world changer. Whether you start a company or join a company, its success is always shared by all of the participating members of the organization.

When sports organizations win championships, the whole club gets rings, from the coach to the secretary. Why? Despite the fact that the secretary never participated in the games, she played a pivotal role in the day-to-day success of the organization.

Developing your team will be one of the most important decisions you will ever make. There are many talented individuals, but ultimately, your team will define your long-term success. For every Bill Gates, there is another witty invention that did not sell because of the inventor's lack of opportunity and connections. For every Michael Jordan, there is a kid who is surrounding himself with people who are blocking doors of opportunity for him to market himself in a greater light. Why? Because whomever you allow in your circle of influence will either help or hurt your dream. There is not any middle ground. It is all or nothing! If you have a glass of water, and you place one drop of poison in it, it is no longer drinkable. One drop changed something that was once pure into poison. This can be said for the people with whom you surround yourself with. Either they are pushing you forward, or they are turning your water into poison.

For each decision you make, there is a positive, neutral, or negative result that is possible. Therefore, there is a higher probability that you will either stay the same or go backwards (negative). Two-thirds of all your choices have either no effect or a negative effect. Therefore, it can be said that only one-third of your choices will move you forward. Wow! How many choices did Oprah, Bill Gates, and Michael Jordan make before they were catapulted forward?

YOUR VIEW

Statistics say that about nine out of every ten businesses fail. With this being true, why not just start ten businesses, if all you need is for one of them to be successful? It is not about how you start, in other words, poor surroundings, lack of parental role models, or lack of opportunity. It is only about how you choose to finish. Either you are a sheep or a lion. It is your choice!

The dreams of your youth are the opportunities of your tomorrow.

If you have a team of misfits around you, you will ultimately be viewed as a misfit, no matter how good of a person you are.

Bill Gates, Oprah Winfrey, and Michael Jordan have established patterns that can be tweaked here and there to fit your goals, but ultimately, the pattern is still the same.

Whatever consumes your time dictates your future.

Take your individual gifts and desires and align them with people to form a team that will give you a higher chance of success.

Begin to look at your dreams. Then, look at your inner circle. Ask yourself, "What around me does not resemble where I want to be?" If you notice that you have people around you that do not resemble the goals you have, you do not have to eliminate those relationships, but it is time to begin to look for new team members who resemble your dream. Either you can choose to move forward, keep it the same, or pull back; ultimately, it is your choice. The decisions you make now pertaining to your team members will have a great effect on your dream in the future.

Newton's Law states, "...that every action has an equal and opposite reaction." What actions are you taking today to position yourself for tomorrow?

PERSONAL NOTES CHAPTER FIVE

_____

_____

_____

_____

_____

_____

_____

_____

_____

_____

_____

_____

_____

_____

_____

_____

_____

_____

_____

CHAPTER SIX
YOUR SURROUNDINGS

*Surroundings (n): environing things, circum-
stances, conditions, etc.; environment[16]*

I have been in many different environments, and although I believe it is important, history has shown that a
dream can supersede any environment. All you need
is clear direction and the willingness to pursue it (your
dream) relentlessly; the rest will be history. There are
thousands of inner-cities across the world from Chicago,
Illinois, to Los Angeles, California; from Beijing, China to
Accra, Ghana. Every day, people are murdered there
or die there. However, in these same places, every day
a child is born that is destined to overcome his or her environment.

I recently was able to travel to Ghana, West Africa, and
while there I had the opportunity to sit down with the Min-
ister of Health. I was amazed at how something as small
as a mosquito (something most Westerners overlook) was
killing so many Africans daily by infecting them with Malaria. For this reason, hundreds if not thousands of children in Africa have the desire to become doctors and/or
scientists, not because it is cool, but because they hope
to be able to discover a cure to prevent Malaria from
continuing to affect the people in their country.

In every environment, there are elements that motivate
the next generation. It is those elements that provide our
deepest levels of motivation. When someone witnesses

41

someone close to them addicted to drugs, or struggling with alcoholism, it creates a burning desire not only for themselves, but to help others from having to go through what they witnessed/lived. Those moments help us develop not only a passion, but a appreciation for those who are victoriously combating the same issues we have either faced or overcame.

Your surroundings or economic situation are only as limiting as you allow them to be.

Most of us go about our daily lives never truly appreciating the simple things. However, in certain parts of the world, young people wish they had half of the opportunities many Americans do not even appreciate.

BOOKS

How many books have you read in the last six months that pertain to your dream? If you cannot remember, or the number is not that high, then do not be upset. Simply go to your nearest library and start checking out those books that will lead you to the fulfillment of your dream.

If you want to travel, find a book and travel through the pages until you are able to travel. Books provide experiences that only words can bring to life. Many of us watch television (myself included) far too much. There is not anything wrong with watching television, but it is someone else's vision (tell-you a vision - television). If you are a dreamer, your dreams should supersede those of a fictional screen.

It's better to start late then to never start at all.

If you want to be doctor, there are thousands of books to choose from that will keep you focused while educating you on the process of what it will take to become a doctor. Also, if you want to be a professional athlete, there are numerous books that teach you how to train and prepare for any sport. No matter what your dream is, there is a book to help you in your journey of reaching your dream. However, books are not the only way of learning. There are movies, lectures, community mentors, and many other opportunities for you to escape your surroundings. However, in order to do so, you must avail yourself of what is out there. No one can do it for you.

Changing your surroundings without changing your outlook is like putting lipstick on a pig. It may look good for the time, but in the end it is still a pig.

1ST CHANCE

When I was 12 years old, living outside of Chicago, Illinois, in a town called Maywood, my grandparents thought that it would be a good idea for me to attend a Christian school in the suburbs. With much excitement, I eagerly anticipated new friendships and the possibility to start over. To my great shock, I found out a life truth: Changing your environment only matters if you change your outlook on your situation.

My perceptions never changed, so despite being in a "better school system," I did not excel. Why? Because I did not embrace my new surroundings. I would rather have been perceived as an inner-city kid than a suburban Christian school student. I did not change my perception; therefore, I missed an opportunity. I was surrounded by kids who seemed to be more determined to get good grades than the friends with whom I had grown up with. I was in a completely different environment, but I could not see the opportunity before me because I was holding onto my old way of life. The opportunity was right in front of me, but I choose to hold on to something that I originally wanted to get out of: the inner-city. I felt like a fish out of water, struggling to find my confront zone.

No matter if you change environments or not, if you do not change your old ways, it will ultimately result in the same outcome.

My advice to you is not to allow yourself to ever miss an opportunity to move forward, because it may never come again.

This is what happens when we let our environment have more influence over us than it should. Therefore, we miss opportunities and do not even realize that everyone is not lucky enough to have opportunities repeat themselves. The truth came out when I had a chance to move forward. I rebelled, just as many still do today. We have opportunities to move closer to our dreams, but because of fear and false realities, we miss them.

TRUE FRIENDS

Many times we try to impress our friends, not knowing that they wish they could have had the opportunities we did.

I have learned that if you set your goals short, or try to impress your peers, you will soon find out that it was not what you wanted after all. Therefore, do not limit yourself.

TOTAL PICTURE

Your surroundings are not just limited to your neighborhood, but also to your friends, family, and more importantly to your perception of your situation and how you will overcome it. Whether the glass is half-full or half-empty does not make any difference; it still has water in it. Many would complain because it is not full, but those with the right perspective will be thankful that they have water to drink. This is a different perception. It is a different way of perceiving both your potential and your situation. See the half glass of water as a gift and not as a right, and you will

Aim for the stars, so that if you fall short, you will still be in space.

make the most out of what you have.

You have to make the most of your situations. If you look at something long enough, you will find flaws; however, your job is not to focus on the flaws, but to appreciate the beauty of the situation. It is then that you will begin to see things for what they are, either stepping stones or trampolines, but never allow anything to pull you backwards.

STATISTICS

This philosophy is the answer to those in situations where the statistics say you are not supposed to succeed and surpass minimal goals. Whether you want to be an athlete, doctor, or a lawyer, use those statistics to motivate you when you do not feel like moving forward. Find those statistics, put them on your wall, and as you break them, check each one off your list. One by one, you will begin to see small victories add up to big victories, which will help motivate you to reach your long-term dreams.

THE NEXT GENERATION

I was not the first, nor will I be the last kid that decides to overcome his environment to become a living dream, and you won't be either. We all have things that we have overcome or are about to overcome, no matter what environment you grew up in, whether it is drugs and gangs, or alcoholism and abuse. We all have a background, but when it comes to the fulfillment of your dreams, ultimately the ball is in your hands as it pertains to education and making good choices.

I must be honest. I know that many people always look for the quick answer: drugs, gangs, cheating on a test, or pushing someone else down so that they can succeed. All of those are quick fixes that will inevitably expose you, and may or may not have long-term effects on your ability to reach your goals.

I have watched two very close friends become victims

Visionaries always see further than what their realities are showing them.

of the quick fixes. It is not a good feeling. I made my mind up a long time ago that I was going to make it, no matter who or what stood in my way. No matter what my surroundings threw at me, I always kept the right perspective. You have to determine whether or not you will allow your surroundings to dictate you, or if you will dictate them.

Visionaries have an uncanny ability to find a way to move forward even when everything else is saying they should halt. Each person reading this book has the potential to do and go farther then those before him or her. All you have to do is take the previous generation's knowledge and develop a clear plan of action that fits your goals and skills. Then, step out in faith.

The first battle is in your thoughts; and from there, your actions will either move you forward or hold you back. When doubt and fear try to make you want to quit, settle it in your heart, and say to yourself that no matter the cost, I will make it.

MIND

You must take control of what you perceive, or you will not be able to determine whether the choices facing you are good or bad.

Conquering your mind will be your biggest challenge. That is why it is important to make sure that you have a written plan of action, so that when doubt comes, and it will, you have something to which to refer. Do not allow yourself to cut your goals short. Your future is at stake. There are no overnight successes. As I once heard it said, "An overnight success was years in the making."

"Your outlook upon life, your estimate of yourself, your estimate of your value is largely colored by your environment. Your whole career will be modified, shaped, and molded by your surroundings, by the character of the people with whom you come in contact every day...." - Orison Swett Marden[17]

Therefore, ensure your success by assembling the right team of people to help you fulfill all your goals, so that your purpose is completed and your surroundings are transformed.

No matter the cost, I will make it.

PERSONAL NOTES CHAPTER SIX

CHAPTER SEVEN
YOUR FOUNDATION

Foundation (n): the basis or groundwork of anything[18]

Every place, team, job, and person you meet is the beginning of a foundation. How you build it determines if the relationship, place, job, or team will be able to handle the added weight of life. If your foundation is solid, it can support whatever opportunities that may arise.

Whenever something is not moving you forward, you must step back and reevaluate it.

THREE LITTLE PIGS

In nursery school, many of us were taught the story of the three little pigs. We must never forget the daily truths of the story. Because of our inability to build solid foundations (brick homes), when the big bad wolf (lifes adversities) comes to blow our houses down, everything we have established quickly scatters in the wind.

LEADER, OR...?

As mentioned before, many people allow statistics to determine their destiny. However, statistics should not be anything more than a motivational tool to reach your dreams. How you develop your foundation will allow you to solidify and expose anything that could be potentially harmful to the fulfillment of your dreams. Most of us do not realize that our greatest hindrance to the fulfillment of our dreams is us, not our surroundings, even though they can make it harder. It is us! You have the ability to choose to overcome statistics and be a forerunner, or not.

Have you built solid foundations with the opportunities you have received?

At 28 years of age, I could have easily allowed statistics to dictate my life's outcome. My mother died when I was six, and I did not have any kind of relationship with my biological father until I was in college. Based upon these facts and the statistics that go along with this type of situation, I should have dropped out of school, ended up in jail, and been a failure in life. The writers of statistics provided me with extra motivation to establish my own path in life, the "right" path. I was able to press past "the statistic," my surroundings and any other type of negativity.

Your success is determined by one thing: you. Yes, your situation plays a part in the way you view and handle things, but ultimately, you make the final decisions. You have the choice to study when your friends are hanging out, or to read instead of watching television. Life is full of choices, and your choices determine your successes and/or failures. Every day you have to make a conscious decision to make choices that will move you a step closer to your dreams, and several steps away from the things that will hold you back and pull you off course.

Plan to be a record breaker, not an average Joe.

Your success is established by the principles that you develop when you are younger. Those principles will follow you throughout your life. If they are not solid when the winds of life blow, everything that you think is valuable will scatter to the wind.

There is a saying, "easy come, easy go," which means that things that come easy go fast; they do not last. In other words, a foundation (which takes time) needs to be built

Short lived success is no success at all.

before your success happens. If it is not solid, as stated earlier, it will crumble, and everything you have worked for will be gone right before your eyes.

GIVING BACK

I strongly believe in planting good seeds into where you want to have success. For example, if you are a lawyer, then help the next generation of desiring lawyers. You will have a deeper rolodex, but also you never know if the one person you help will happen to be the one to carry the torch for you after your days are over. In helping someone else, you will find a joy that very few people have the pleasure to experience. As you mentor or help someone else through the journey that you once traveled to enter your career, you will begin to understand at a greater level why your journey was so important that only you could have completed it. Every struggle and hard life lesson you had to endure will all begin to make greater sense.

The roads we travel in life are bumpy not just to teach us lessons, but also so that we can share our lessons learned with those who are following us. Whether you write a letter of recommendation or just are the person who encourages people when they become frustrated, it all has purpose.

The average American will live to be 70+ years of age, yet many teenagers allow 12 (K-12th grade) years of their life to dictate the next 50+ years.

Most people move forward and do not look back until they are about to die or retire (some might argue retirement is death). Then, they scramble to find something to fill what already could have been filled if they would have given back along the way.

BILL GATES, A PROTOTYPE

Bill Gates started his foundation years before he decided to step down from the day-to-day activities of Microsoft. By doing that, I truly believe that his transition after Microsoft was easier. He did not have to scramble to find something to fill the void of working long hours at Microsoft. I also believe that his legacy will not be determined by his accomplishments at Microsoft, despite how great and financially rewarding they were. Rather, I believe the reach of his foundation (the Bill & Melinda Gates Foundation) will be felt around the world for years to come because of the opportunities it is presenting to underserved countries and communities.

Success - (an) achievement of something desired, planned or attempted[19]

THE FRUIT OF LABOR - MONEY!

I would be remiss if I didn't warn you about money. All of your goals will bring some form of riches. You must educate yourself in the language of money. If not, you will not be able to speak and understand whether or not someone has your best interests at heart. When it comes to money, always ask, seek, and knock. Always ask yourself, does this fit into my overall plan? Then, seek out understanding to determine if the reward justifies the risk. Lastly, knock on the doors of those who have gone before you. Find people who have been successful with money. Remember, you

Good grades and dreams go hand-in-hand. Great students have doors opened for them, while everyone else is wondering why they receive special treatment.

wouldn't go to a plumber and ask for help with your cable, so do not treat your money with a lesser value then you would your cable.

All goals have the potential to bring rewards. You must not focus on the rewards, but instead focus on the six P's of success: proper prior planning prevents poor performance.[20] This way, when the doors open, you are ready, able, and willing to walk through them, knowing your foundation is secure.

REMEMBER

Money is neither good nor bad. It only takes on the character of the person who has it. Therefore, make sure your foundation is solid, so that the generations that follow you will be eternally grateful.

PERSONAL NOTES CHAPTER SEVEN

_____

_____

_____

_____

_____

_____

_____

_____

_____

_____

_____

_____

_____

_____

_____

_____

_____

_____

_____

_____

FOOD FOR THOUGHT

The more money one has often leads to a greater level of accountability.

You must make sure your team holds you accountable at all times.

These are the questions you should be asking yourself long before you ever graduate from college.

The bigger the decision, the more I research.

Dreamers never stop dreaming until all their dreams either come to pass or pass them by.

Always value whatever you have, and just because you can dream it, does not mean you have to buy it.

Do what you have to do, so you can do what you want to do.

You can never live on another man's understanding. You must be willing to find out for yourself.

Despite having a plan of action, you must always be prepared for the unexpected.

Words without proof are worthless, but words with action (proof) are priceless.

Prepare not only for today, but weigh it for tomorrow.

You cannot have passion without purpose being either

there, or at the door waiting to enter.

When you commit to your dreams, there is nothing else.

Oftentimes we think that our dreams are our purpose, and oftentimes they are not.

Always enjoy your success, because in life, everything has a beginning and an end.

No matter how bleak a situation, there is always light if you look hard enough.

Successful people understand how to create patterns of success.

Dreams shift mindsets, and mindsets control environments. So, if you can shift minds, you can ultimately shift environments.

There are no shortcuts to reaching any dream worth fulfilling.

When you are giving back, always check your motives, because if they are not pure, it will prevent you from being productive in mentoring good leaders.

I am not writing this book off another man's knowledge or research alone. I have lived this. I have made good and bad choices. The only difference is that I have had an opportunity to correct mine. You may or may not be as lucky, so make the most of your choices now.

My definition of team: many different personalities and skills, coming together to form one seamless unit to accomplish one single task.

"I" is only one letter, yet "team" is made up of four.

Never burn bridges or towns, because on the way home you will probably have to put out the fire.

When you give up yourself for the benefit of the team, the team usually prospers more than if you had not given up anything at all.

If you never give up anything, how will you ever have room for more?

The dreams of your youth are opportunities of your tomorrow.

Whatever consumes your time dictates your future.

Your surroundings or economic situation is only as limiting as you allow it to be.

It's better to start late then to never start at all.

Changing your surroundings without changing your outlook is like putting lipstick on a pig. It may look good for the time, but in the end it is still a pig.

No matter if you change environments or not, if you do not change your old ways, it will ultimately result in the same outcome.

My advice to you is not to allow yourself to ever miss an opportunity to move forward, because it may never come again.

Aim for the stars, so if you fall short, you will still be in space.

Visionaries always see further than what their realities are showing them.

You must take control of what you perceive, or you will not be able to determine whether the choices facing you are good or bad.

No matter the cost, I will make it.

An overnight success was years in the making.

Whenever something is not moving you forward, you must step back and reevaluate it.

Have you built solid foundations with the opportunities you have received?

Short lived success is no success at all.

The average American will live to be 70+ years of age, yet many teenagers allow 12 (K-12th grade) years of their life to dictate the next 50+ years.

Good grades and dreams go hand-in-hand. Great students have doors opened for them, while everyone else is wondering why they receive special treatment.

Plan to be a record breaker, not an average Joe.

DEFINITIONS

Accountability (n): the state of being accountable, liable, or answerable[1]

Wisdom (is) the quality or state of being wise; knowledge of what is true or right coupled with just judgment as to action; sagacity, discernment, or insight[2]

Knowledge (is) the body of truths or facts accumulated in the course of time[3]

Truth (is) conformity with fact or reality; verity[4]

Vision (n): the act or power of anticipating that which will or may come to be[6]

Value- relative worth, merit, or importance[7]

Success (is) the favorable or prosperous termination of attempts or endeavors[8]

Reward (is) something given or received in return or recompense for service, merit, hardship, etc.[9]

Thief (is) a person who steals, esp. secretly or without open force; one guilty of theft or larceny.[10]

Purpose (n): the reason for which something exists or is done, made or used[12]

Dream (n): is a wild fancy hope[13]

Team (n) a number of persons associated in some joint action[14]

Unity - an undivided or unbroken completeness or totality with nothing wanting[15]

Surroundings (n): environing things, circumstances, conditions, etc.; environment[16]

Foundation (n) the basis or groundwork of anything[18]

Success (an) achievement of something desired, planned, or attempted[19]

NOTES

Chapter One
Accountability

1. Dictionary.com, s.v. "Accountability," http://dictionary.reference.com/browse/accountability (accessed November 9, 2010).

2. Dictionary.com, s.v. "Wisdom," http://dictionary.reference.com/browse/wisdom(accessed November 9, 2010).

3. Dictionary.com, s.v. "Knowledge," http://dictionary.reference.com/browse/knowledge (accessed November 9, 2010).

4. Dictionary.com, s.v. "Truth," http://dictionary.reference.com/browse/ truth (accessed November 9, 2010).

5. Thinkexist.com, "Stephen R. Covey," http://thinkexist.com/quotation/accountability_breeds_response-ability/297755.html (accessed November 9, 2010).

Chapter Two
Vision

6. Dictionary.com, s.v. "Vision," http://dictionary.reference.com/browse/vision (accessed November 9, 2010).

7. Dictionary.com, s.v. "Value," http://dictionary.reference.com/browse/value (accessed November 9, 2010).

8. Dictionary.com, s.v. "Success," http://dictionary.reference.com/browse/success (accessed November 9, 2010).

9. Dictionary.com, s.v. "Reward," http://dictionary.reference.com/browse/reward (accessed November 9, 2010).

10. Dictionary.com, s.v. "Thief," http://dictionary.reference.com/browse/thief (accessed November 9, 2010).

11. Quotes4all.net, "Henry Ford," http://quotes4all.net/henry%20ford.html (accessed November 9, 2010)

Chapter Three
Purpose

12. Dictionary.com, s.v. "Purpose," http://dictionary.reference.com/browse/purpose (accessed November 9, 2010).

Chapter Four
Dreams

13. Dictionary.com, s.v. "Dream," http://dictionary.reference.com/browse/dream (accessed November 9, 2010).

Chapter Five
Your Team

14. Dictionary.com, s.v. "Team," http://dictionary.reference.com/browse/team (accessed November 9, 2010).

15. Dictionary.com, s.v. "Unity," http://dictionary. reference.com/browse/unity (accessed November 9, 2010).

Chapter Six
Your Surroundings

16. Dictionary.com, s.v. "Surroundings," http://dictionary. reference.com/browse/surroundings (accessed November 9, 2010).

17. Brainyquote.com, s.v. "Orison Swett Marden," http://www.brainyquote.com/quotes/quotes/o/ orisonswet157891.html (accessed November 9, 2010).

Chapter Seven
Your Foundation

18. Dictionary.com, s.v. "Foundation," http://dictionary. reference.com/browse/foundation (accessed November 9, 2010).

19. Dictionary.com, s.v. "Success," http://dictionary. reference.com/browse/success (accessed November 9, 2010).

20. Wikipedia.com, "6 P's," http://en.wikipedia.org/ wiki/7_Ps_(military_adage)#The_6_Ps (accessed November 9 2010)

PASSION_{to}PURPOSE™

Please feel free to write and share how this book has helped you, and forward it to:
info@passtopurpose.com

If you want to receive emails and updates as to when I will be in your area, please visit
www.passtopurpose.com

CPSIA information can be obtained
at www.ICGtesting.com
Printed in the USA
FFOW03n2323030717
37380FF